THE DISCIPLE'S

JOURNAL

A MULTIPURPOSE SPIRITUAL JOURNAL

This journal belongs to:

Name: _____

Address: _____

Phone: _____

Email: _____

Journal Period: _____

"Go therefore and make disciples of all the nations, baptizing them in the name
of the Father and of the Son and of the Holy Spirit"
Matthew 28:19

THE DISCIPLE'S

JOURNAL

A MULTIPURPOSE SPIRITUAL JOURNAL

CHRISTINE L. EDWARDS

The Disciple's Journal, A Multipurpose Spiritual Journal
Published by Christine L. Edwards
P.O. Box 1152
White River Junction, Vermont 05001
www..christineledwards.com

Editors: Caitlin Jula, BookBaby editing services
Cover Photo: Nik Shuliahin on Unsplash.com
Cover Design: Christine L. Edwards
Interior Design: Christine L. Edwards
Author Photo: Beverly TessJohnson

ISBN-13: 978-0-692-19089-0

Dedicated to:

My precious Savior Jesus! Without Him I have nothing.

Each person who uses this journal. May it stir up the spiritual gifts in you, and inspire you to be all God has destined you to be.

My loving husband, John Delbert Edwards, whose love and support have been a priceless gift. Thank you for showing me the steadfastness of a Godly man.

Karissa, Kaitlynn, and Jaiden. May you know the love of Christ in abundant measure. I'm so blessed that God chose me to be your mother. It has been a privilege and a delight!

To my mother, Beverly, for making the decision to step beyond religion and introduce our family to a relationship with Jesus.

The J's (Jula) and the B's (Binford) of the JEB's. Your support, prayers, and continual challenges to grow in faith have meant the world to me. You have been such a blessing to my family!

<u>Contents</u>

Introduction

Welcome to *The Disciple's Journal.* My hope is that this journal starts you on an exciting journey of spiritual growth that not only changes your life but also affects the lives of those around you as well.

Let me tell you a little bit of my story and how *The Disciple's Journal* came to be.

I have been a born-again Christian since the age of twelve, but did not really get serious about my faith and personal walk with the Lord until I was about thirty-two years old. At that point in my life, I decided I was all in when it came to God after having strayed for several years. I recommitted my life to Jesus and began attending church again on a regular basis. I served in the church, began reading my Bible each day, and started keeping a journal. A few years later I decided to attend the ministry school run by my church, which propelled me into an even deeper commitment to my walk with the Lord.

I excelled in my studies in ministry school and experienced tremendous spiritual growth during that time. I believe my success was in part because I have always been a very studious person. I love to learn! I would frequently take notes on things I read, sermons I listened to, and random things I felt the Lord was speaking to me. Often these things that ministered to me and ignited something in my spirit. Other times, they would be helpful for someone I knew.

However, as the years passed, I began to feel frustrated that I hadn't made as much progress in my spiritual walk as I would have liked. It wasn't for a lack of seeking Him - it was primarily because of a lack of follow-through on my part. One day, as I looked at the haphazard piles of scribbled notes I had written and journals I had started or filled during the course of my daily life, one thing became very clear: My writings and ideas were disorganized and not producing the life changes I desired. In this mess of paper, I had great ideas, things I felt God wanted me to do, and areas in my life God wanted me to address. However, there was a major issue: Few of these thoughtfully written notes ever made it past the paper they were written on to practical application and true life changes.

This was a sad moment for me. My heart was broken over this revelation. Thankfully, God is faithful and docs not give us revelation without providing us wisdom on how to move forward. Through His perfect love and grace, then, that revelation also brought me great hope and pure joy!

As I began to pray for such wisdom on how to address this issue, it occurred to me that I am not alone. Others out there have this same struggle. I realized that in helping myself, I would be able to help others as well, and how better could I honor God than in sharing with others the insight He has given me!

My heart desires to be a true disciple and to fulfill the calling that God has for my life. I realized that to do that, I needed to find a way to get past the obstacle that was hindering me from seeing the tangible spiritual growth and life changes I desired. I needed to get organized and take action on the things God wanted me to do.

This journal is a tool to assist you in moving past the obstacle in your own life. Imagine the changes you will see in your life as you become a better steward over what God has called you to do!

It may also cause a ripple effect and inspire those around you.

For organizational purposes, this journal is broken down into the following five sections:

- Spiritual Journal
- Dream Journal
- Prayer Journal
- Gratitude Journal
- Memorable Moments Journal

At the beginning of each journal section I have shared how I use it for my own spiritual walk. If you are new to journaling, you may find this helpful in getting you started. If you are a seasoned journal keeper, then it may just prompt you to switch things up a little bit and try something different. It is in no way meant to be a formula you must follow. Let the Holy Spirit lead you – that is always the best way!

I love that this journal has gotten me organized! I no longer have multiple journals and piles of random notes hanging around. It has also made it much easier to find things I have written down when I want to reflect on them later.

Use this journal as it works best for you. I tend to write a lot, so I use a new journal each year. But if you write only a little, that's fine! One journal may last you a couple of years. I do suggest that you date all your journal entries. Having dates on them can provide additional insight when reflecting upon them months or years from when you originally wrote them. When your journal is full, record the period the journal covers in the front of your journal.

As you keep these dated journals, you are also creating a spiritual legacy. I love the thought that one day my children and grandchildren will be able to read about all the trials and joys of my spiritual journey and glean insights from what I have walked through.

I pray this journal will be a tool to help you cultivate your relationship with the Lord. May it strengthen your resolve to be a person of influence and integrity for His glory as you activate your potential and step into all He has called you to do. Let us not be just hearers of the Word, but let us also be doers of the Word. May our actions speak louder than our words, and may we be a catalyst for change in our own lives, communities, and nations.. In Jesus' name, Amen.

In Pursuit of Jesus,

Christine

Spiritual Journal

Our personal relationship with God is the most important aspect of our lives. Since becoming truly devoted to a relationship with God, I have continually been in pursuit of a deeper intimacy with Him.

Despite being involved in church, reading my Bible, and spending time in prayer, I reached a point in my spiritual walk where I was frustrated and feeling spiritually stagnant. God gave me revelation that one of the reasons for this sense of frustration and stagnation was my lack of follow-through on things He had laid on my heart to do.

One morning as I was praying, the Lord gave me the acronym H.O.P.E. (Highlight, Observe, Pray, Engage). Applying this acronym to my spiritual journal entries has helped me tremendously. By doing so, not only do I have a record of what He is speaking to me, but I also have an action plan to help me follow through on what God is asking me to do.

So, let's break it down this acronym.

HIGHLIGHT

When I refer to the term **highlight**, I am talking about things that spark something in your spirit. It may be something that ignites a passion in you, brings revelation, kindles inspiration, or illuminates a newfound direction or purpose for your life. These things may come from a sermon, Scripture, a book, or a prophetic word someone has given you.

Think of it as using a highlighter. Many of us have used highlighters because something has stood out to us in books or our Bibles. If you are anything like me, you also scribble down notes on paper during sermons, or about something significant someone has said to you that you want to remember. These are all highlights. If you would highlight it, underline it, or write it down as important, then this is your highlight item for your journal entry.

Writing out your highlight is the first step. It can be as brief or as detailed as you need it to be, but it is always a good idea to note the date and the source of the highlight in case you need to go back and reference it later.

OBSERVE

The second step is **observe**. This is what you have personally taken away from that highlight you recorded in the first step. What thoughts, revelation, or feelings were stirred by it? What did you learn from it? Perhaps the highlight has left you with more questions than you had to start with. That's okay! Such a realization can be an observation as well. This is where you will note all those things.

PRAY

The next step is to **pray** about it. Seek the Lord and ask Him if there is something you need to do in reference to what has been revealed to you. Share your heart with Him on the matter. Here you can write out your prayers and the answers you receive.

Answers are not always immediate. That's a normal part of pursuing God. Sometimes we have to be persistent in our prayers and listen intently before the Lord reveals our next steps to us. You can always come back and finish your H.O.P.E. spiritual journal entry when God does speak something to you. Just be sure to leave some space so that you can add to your journal entry later.

Of course there may be times when there is nothing specific you need to do in regards to the highlight. In that case stop here at H.O.P., and hop on over to your next journal highlight.

ENGAGE

The last step is **engage**! Here is where the rubber meets the road so to speak. This is where real life changes and spiritual growth can accelerate.

How you can take what you have learned or what has been revealed to you and apply it to your life?

When we engage with something, we accompany it from being a good thought or idea to becoming something more tangible. We put things in motion, we get involved, and we begin to change ourselves and influence those around us.

Once you have an idea how to implement this new action or idea in your life, set aside the time to actually do it. Put it on your calendar! Make the commitment to follow through with it.

But do you want to know, O foolish man, that faith without works is dead?
James 2:20

Here is an example of one of my H.O.P.E. spiritual journal entries to provide you with a little guidance and inspiration:

H.O.P.E. (Highlight Observe Pray Engage)   May 8, 2018
Notes from a sermon by Pastor Steven Furtick titled "Talk Yourself Into It" - available on YouTube.

Highlight -

- Just because I have fear doesn't mean fear has to have me.
- My real enemies are fear and discouragement.
- What have I talked myself out of that God is trying to bring me into?
- Stop forfeiting my future for fear of people and/or fear of failure.
- Nobody can talk me into my destiny but me.
- Learning to encourage myself is a sign of spiritual maturity.
- My courage comes from the conversations I have with myself - so does my fear
- Stop listening to myself think or talk about a situation and start preaching to it!
- Christ is in me! I am enough!

Observe - When I look back on my life I can easily see this familiar pattern: I have an idea or a hope for something I want to see take place in my life and I let fear of what others will think about me, fear of failure, or feeling unqualified stop me from moving forward. I often talk myself out of things based on fear or my own assumptions. Sometimes I also slip into comparing myself or my qualifications or abilities with others, which further solidifies why I believe I am unqualified to do something. For my life to change, this pattern must change! I need to learn to overcome fear, trust God no matter the outcome, learn to encourage myself, and begin talking myself into things rather than out of them.

Pray – God, I thank you for the revelation You bring and for timely messages such as these. I repent of all the times I have talked myself out of something You have tried to bring me in to. This is an area in my life that I want to see changed. Please guide me as I do the work in the areas I need to and as I allow You full access to work on the my heart as You need to. Together we can overcome this hurdle in my life so that I can walk in the fullness of my calling and destiny. Amen.

Engage - Write down my fears and face them. Be completely honest! If I were giving advice to a friend on those fears, what would I tell them? Follow my own advice! Create some talk-myself-into-it statements to rehearse daily and read when I need to start talking to myself instead of listening to myself. Include Scriptures - there is power in the Word - wield your sword MIGHTY WARRIOR! Complete by 5/15/18.

Spiritual Journal - H.O.P.E. (Highlight Observe Pray Engage)

Spiritual Journal - H.O.P.E. (Highlight Observe Pray Engage)

_____

_____

_____

_____

_____

_____

_____

_____

_____

_____

_____

_____

_____

_____

_____

_____

_____

_____

_____

_____

_____

Spiritual Journal - H.O.P.E. (Highlight Observe Pray Engage)

Spiritual Journal - H.O.P.E. (Highlight Observe Pray Engage)

_____

_____

_____

_____

_____

_____

_____

_____

_____

_____

_____

_____

_____

_____

_____

_____

_____

_____

_____

_____

_____

Spiritual Journal - H.O.P.E. (Highlight Observe Pray Engage)

_____

_____

_____

_____

_____

_____

_____

_____

_____

_____

_____

_____

_____

_____

_____

_____

_____

_____

_____

_____

Spiritual Journal - H.O.P.E. (Highlight Observe Pray Engage)

Spiritual Journal - H.O.P.E. (Highlight Observe Pray Engage)

_____

_____

_____

_____

_____

_____

_____

_____

_____

_____

_____

_____

_____

_____

_____

_____

_____

_____

_____

_____

_____

Spiritual Journal - H.O.P.E. (Highlight Observe Pray Engage)

_____

_____

_____

_____

_____

_____

_____

_____

_____

_____

_____

_____

_____

_____

_____

_____

_____

_____

_____

Spiritual Journal - H.O.P.E. (Highlight Observe Pray Engage)

Spiritual Journal - H.O.P.E. (Highlight Observe Pray Engage)

_____

_____

_____

_____

_____

_____

_____

_____

_____

_____

_____

_____

_____

_____

_____

_____

_____

_____

_____

_____

_____

Spiritual Journal - H.O.P.E. (Highlight Observe Pray Engage)

Spiritual Journal - H.O.P.E. (Highlight Observe Pray Engage)

_____

_____

_____

_____

_____

_____

_____

_____

_____

_____

_____

_____

_____

_____

_____

_____

_____

_____

_____

_____

Spiritual Journal - H.O.P.E. (Highlight Observe Pray Engage)

_____

_____

_____

_____

_____

_____

_____

_____

_____

_____

_____

_____

_____

_____

_____

_____

_____

_____

_____

_____

_____

Spiritual Journal - H.O.P.E. (Highlight Observe Pray Engage)

_____

_____

_____

_____

_____

_____

_____

_____

_____

_____

_____

_____

_____

_____

_____

_____

_____

_____

_____

_____

Spiritual Journal - H.O.P.E. (Highlight Observe Pray Engage)

_____

_____

_____

_____

_____

_____

_____

_____

_____

_____

_____

_____

_____

_____

_____

_____

_____

_____

_____

_____

_____

Spiritual Journal - H.O.P.E. (Highlight Observe Pray Engage)

_____

_____

_____

_____

_____

_____

_____

_____

_____

_____

_____

_____

_____

_____

_____

_____

_____

_____

_____

_____

_____

Spiritual Journal - H.O.P.E. (Highlight Observe Pray Engage)

_____

_____

_____

_____

_____

_____

_____

_____

_____

_____

_____

_____

_____

_____

_____

_____

_____

_____

_____

_____

_____

Spiritual Journal - H.O.P.E. (Highlight Observe Pray Engage)

_____

_____

_____

_____

_____

_____

_____

_____

_____

_____

_____

_____

_____

_____

_____

_____

_____

_____

_____

_____

Spiritual Journal - H.O.P.E. (Highlight Observe Pray Engage)

Spiritual Journal - H.O.P.E. (Highlight Observe Pray Engage)

_____

_____

_____

_____

_____

_____

_____

_____

_____

_____

_____

_____

_____

_____

_____

_____

_____

_____

_____

_____

_____

Spiritual Journal - H.O.P.E. (Highlight Observe Pray Engage)

_____

_____

_____

_____

_____

_____

_____

_____

_____

_____

_____

_____

_____

_____

_____

_____

_____

_____

_____

_____

_____

Spiritual Journal - H.O.P.E. (Highlight Observe Pray Engage)

_____

_____

_____

_____

_____

_____

_____

_____

_____

_____

_____

_____

_____

_____

_____

_____

_____

_____

_____

_____

_____

Spiritual Journal - H.O.P.E. (Highlight Observe Pray Engage)

_____

_____

_____

_____

_____

_____

_____

_____

_____

_____

_____

_____

_____

_____

_____

_____

_____

_____

_____

_____

Spiritual Journal - H.O.P.E. (Highlight Observe Pray Engage)

_____

_____

_____

_____

_____

_____

_____

_____

_____

_____

_____

_____

_____

_____

_____

_____

_____

_____

_____

_____

_____

_____

Spiritual Journal - H.O.P.E. (Highlight Observe Pray Engage)

_____

_____

_____

_____

_____

_____

_____

_____

_____

_____

_____

_____

_____

_____

_____

_____

_____

_____

_____

_____

Spiritual Journal - H.O.P.E. (Highlight Observe Pray Engage)

_____

_____

_____

_____

_____

_____

_____

_____

_____

_____

_____

_____

_____

_____

_____

_____

_____

_____

Spiritual Journal - H.O.P.E. (Highlight Observe Pray Engage)

_____

_____

_____

_____

_____

_____

_____

_____

_____

_____

_____

_____

_____

_____

_____

_____

_____

_____

_____

_____

_____

_____

Spiritual Journal - H.O.P.E. (Highlight Observe Pray Engage)

_____

_____

_____

_____

_____

_____

_____

_____

_____

_____

_____

_____

_____

_____

_____

_____

_____

_____

_____

_____

_____

_____

Spiritual Journal - H.O.P.E. (Highlight Observe Pray Engage)

_____

_____

_____

_____

_____

_____

_____

_____

_____

_____

_____

_____

_____

_____

_____

_____

_____

_____

_____

_____

_____

_____

_____

Spiritual Journal - H.O.P.E. (Highlight Observe Pray Engage)

_____

_____

_____

_____

_____

_____

_____

_____

_____

_____

_____

_____

_____

_____

_____

_____

_____

_____

_____

_____

_____

Spiritual Journal - H.O.P.E. (Highlight Observe Pray Engage)

_____

_____

_____

_____

_____

_____

_____

_____

_____

_____

_____

_____

_____

_____

_____

_____

_____

_____

_____

_____

_____

Spiritual Journal - H.O.P.E. (Highlight Observe Pray Engage)

_____

_____

_____

_____

_____

_____

_____

_____

_____

_____

_____

_____

_____

_____

_____

_____

_____

_____

_____

_____

Spiritual Journal - H.O.P.E. (Highlight Observe Pray Engage)

_____

_____

_____

_____

_____

_____

_____

_____

_____

_____

_____

_____

_____

_____

_____

_____

_____

_____

_____

_____

_____

_____

Spiritual Journal - H.O.P.E. (Highlight Observe Pray Engage)

Spiritual Journal - H.O.P.E. (Highlight Observe Pray Engage)

_____

_____

_____

_____

_____

_____

_____

_____

_____

_____

_____

_____

_____

_____

_____

_____

_____

_____

_____

_____

Spiritual Journal - H.O.P.E. (Highlight Observe Pray Engage)

Spiritual Journal - H.O.P.E. (Highlight Observe Pray Engage)

Spiritual Journal - H.O.P.E. (Highlight Observe Pray Engage)

Spiritual Journal - H.O.P.E. (Highlight Observe Pray Engage)

_____

_____

_____

_____

_____

_____

_____

_____

_____

_____

_____

_____

_____

_____

_____

_____

_____

_____

_____

Spiritual Journal - H.O.P.E. (Highlight Observe Pray Engage)

Spiritual Journal - H.O.P.E. (Highlight Observe Pray Engage)

_____

_____

_____

_____

_____

_____

_____

_____

_____

_____

_____

_____

_____

_____

_____

_____

_____

_____

_____

_____

Spiritual Journal - H.O.P.E. (Highlight Observe Pray Engage)

Spiritual Journal - H.O.P.E. (Highlight Observe Pray Engage)

_____

_____

_____

_____

_____

_____

_____

_____

_____

_____

_____

_____

_____

_____

_____

_____

_____

_____

_____

_____

Spiritual Journal - H.O.P.E. (Highlight Observe Pray Engage)

_____

_____

_____

_____

_____

_____

_____

_____

_____

_____

_____

_____

_____

_____

_____

_____

_____

_____

_____

_____

_____

Spiritual Journal - H.O.P.E. (Highlight Observe Pray Engage)

Spiritual Journal - H.O.P.E. (Highlight Observe Pray Engage)

_____

_____

_____

_____

_____

_____

_____

_____

_____

_____

_____

_____

_____

_____

_____

_____

_____

_____

_____

_____

_____

_____

Spiritual Journal - H.O.P.E. (Highlight Observe Pray Engage)

Spiritual Journal - H.O.P.E. (Highlight Observe Pray Engage)

_____

_____

_____

_____

_____

_____

_____

_____

_____

_____

_____

_____

_____

_____

_____

_____

_____

_____

_____

_____

Spiritual Journal - H.O.P.E. (Highlight Observe Pray Engage)

_____

_____

_____

_____

_____

_____

_____

_____

_____

_____

_____

_____

_____

_____

_____

_____

_____

_____

_____

_____

Spiritual Journal - H.O.P.E. (Highlight Observe Pray Engage)

_____

_____

_____

_____

_____

_____

_____

_____

_____

_____

_____

_____

_____

_____

_____

_____

_____

_____

_____

_____

_____

Spiritual Journal – H.O.P.E. (Highlight Observe Pray Engage)

Spiritual Journal - H.O.P.E. (Highlight Observe Pray Engage)

_____

_____

_____

_____

_____

_____

_____

_____

_____

_____

_____

_____

_____

_____

_____

_____

_____

_____

_____

_____

_____

_____

Dream Journal

The purpose of this section of the journal is to keep a record of the dreams that you have. In my dream journal I focus on two types of dreams: dreams I have while I am sleeping and my own personal dreams.

Let's talk first about the dreams we have while we are asleep. I never used to pay much attention to my dreams. Some of them were weird and off-the-wall, some were scary, and then there were some that just left me wondering if there was some meaning to them.

Then the day came when one of the dreams I had about someone I barely knew actually happened. Suddenly I began to realize that not all the dreams I had were just to be dismissed so easily as odd or meaningless.

I shared this experience with one of my spiritual mentors, who subsequently put me on a path to discovering how often God spoke to people in dreams in the Bible.

Throughout the Bible, we see where God has spoken to people through dreams. An angel of God spoke to Jacob in a dream in Genesis 31:11; the Lord appeared to Solomon in a dream in 1 Kings 3:5-15; God showed Joseph glimpses of his future in dreams in Genesis 37; and later in Genesis chapters 40 and 41, Joseph interprets the dreams of others. God continued to use dreams to communicate with people in the New Testament. He used dreams to tell Joseph to take Mary as his wife (Matthew 1:20) and even when to flee to Egypt so that Jesus' life would be spared (Matthew 2:13). These are just a few examples in the Bible where God has spoken to people through dreams.

Furthermore, Acts 2:17 says, "And it shall come to pass in the last days, says God, That I will pour out of My Spirit on all flesh; Your sons and your daughters shall prophesy, Your young men shall see visions, Your old men shall dream dreams." So we can continue to expect that God will use dreams as a way of communicating with us.

Record your dreams in this section of the journal. Include the date that you had the dream, the specific details, and any feelings you had as you were dreaming it. Once you have written out the dream pray about it. Ask the Lord to reveal to you the meaning of the dream, what or how He is speaking to you through it, and if there is something specific He wants you to be in prayer about.

Then write down anything He speaks to you. If you don't get any insight on it right away just leave some space to write out any revelations you get later. Sometimes we do not understand the meaning of a dream until months, or in some cases, even years later.

Of course you can also seek out a trusted spiritual mentor or pastor to share your dreams with. There are members of the Body of Christ who are spiritually gifted in the interpretation of dreams and can be a great resource in helping you navigate your dreams.

Now on to dreams that we have for our life. Often God places our heart's desires and dreams there, so this is the perfect place to write out those dreams and aspirations.. Don't be limited by what you think is possible - let your imagination run wild! As big as we can dream, God can always dream bigger. What may be impossible on our own, is totally possible with God!

As you write out these dreams leave plenty of space to add things later as you begin to see how your dreams change or unfold over time.

You can also add an action plan for your dreams. List steps you can take to move toward achieving each dream, and just like the **engage** step in the spiritual journal, begin scheduling time on your calendar to take action on those steps. God will do His part, but we also need to do ours.

But Jesus looked at them and said to them, "With men this is impossible, but with God all things are possible."
Matthew 19:26

Dream Journal

Dream Journal

Dream Journal

Dream Journal

_____

_____

_____

_____

_____

_____

_____

_____

_____

_____

_____

_____

_____

_____

_____

_____

_____

_____

_____

_____

_____

Dream Journal

Dream Journal

Dream Journal

_____

_____

_____

_____

_____

_____

_____

_____

_____

_____

_____

_____

_____

_____

_____

_____

_____

_____

_____

_____

Dream Journal

_____

_____

_____

_____

_____

_____

_____

_____

_____

_____

_____

_____

_____

_____

_____

_____

_____

_____

_____

_____

_____

Dream Journal

Dream Journal

_____

_____

_____

_____

_____

_____

_____

_____

_____

_____

_____

_____

_____

_____

_____

_____

_____

_____

_____

_____

_____

_____

_____

Dream Journal

Dream Journal

Dream Journal

Dream Journal

_____

_____

_____

_____

_____

_____

_____

_____

_____

_____

_____

_____

_____

_____

_____

_____

_____

_____

_____

_____

_____

_____

Dream Journal

Dream Journal

_____

_____

_____

_____

_____

_____

_____

_____

_____

_____

_____

_____

_____

_____

_____

_____

_____

_____

_____

_____

_____

_____

Dream Journal

_____

_____

_____

_____

_____

_____

_____

_____

_____

_____

_____

_____

_____

_____

_____

_____

_____

_____

_____

_____

_____

_____

_____

Dream Journal

_____

_____

_____

_____

_____

_____

_____

_____

_____

_____

_____

_____

_____

_____

_____

_____

_____

_____

_____

_____

_____

_____

Dream Journal

Dream Journal

_____

_____

_____

_____

_____

_____

_____

_____

_____

_____

_____

_____

_____

_____

_____

_____

_____

_____

_____

_____

_____

_____

Dream Journal

Dream Journal

Dream Journal

Dream Journal

Dream Journal

Dream Journal

_____

_____

_____

_____

_____

_____

_____

_____

_____

_____

_____

_____

_____

_____

_____

_____

_____

_____

_____

_____

_____

_____

_____

Dream Journal

_____

_____

_____

_____

_____

_____

_____

_____

_____

_____

_____

_____

_____

_____

_____

_____

_____

_____

_____

_____

_____

Dream Journal

Dream Journal

Dream Journal

Dream Journal

Dream Journal

Dream Journal

Dream Journal

_____

_____

_____

_____

_____

_____

_____

_____

_____

_____

_____

_____

_____

_____

_____

_____

_____

_____

_____

_____

_____

_____

Dream Journal

Dream Journal

_____

_____

_____

_____

_____

_____

_____

_____

_____

_____

_____

_____

_____

_____

_____

_____

_____

_____

_____

_____

_____

Dream Journal

Dream Journal

Dream Journal

_____

_____

_____

_____

_____

_____

_____

_____

_____

_____

_____

_____

_____

_____

_____

_____

_____

_____

_____

_____

_____

_____

Dream Journal

_____

_____

_____

_____

_____

_____

_____

_____

_____

_____

_____

_____

_____

_____

_____

_____

_____

_____

_____

_____

_____

_____

Dream Journal

Prayer Journal

When it came to my prayer life I really needed some help! I do not know if you can relate to this, but while I can easily remember things I am keeping in prayer for myself or for those closest to me, there are times I am not good at remembering to pray for others.

I frequently get messages from people asking for prayer or someone in person asking for prayer in passing. I tell them that I will pray for them, and I mean it with all sincerity. However, all too often, unless I do it at that very moment, I end up forgetting and remember my promise only days later or the next time I see them. I then end up feeling bad about having forgotten. Am I alone in this, or do you have this same problem from time to time?

To help me with this, I created a prayer journal. It not only helps me to remember the prayer requests of others, but it also helps me to remember to follow up with them, see how they are doing , and ask if they have seen an answer to their prayers yet.

The benefit is not just for the person I am praying for. It also builds my faith! When I see how God has answered my prayers and the prayers of others, it builds my faith and encourages me to know that prayer does work!

For those prayers that seem to go unanswered, this practice and feedback gives me endurance to keep pressing on. To keep seeking God, keep praying and keep expecting.

In this section write down things you are keeping in prayer for yourself or for others. Date your entries and leave space between the prayers to record how God answered those prayers.

Sometimes answers are delayed for long periods of time, and other times prayers may be answered quickly. God's timing is not our own. He knows when the best time is to answer a prayer. When answers are delayed, you may also want to record what you learned while you were waiting for the answer to come. How did you grow spiritually by having to wait for God to answer the prayer?

I have found that keeping a prayer journal has not only helped focus my prayer life, it has also increased my desire to pray more and grow more deeply in intimacy with God.

Rejoice always, pray without ceasing, in everything gift thanks; for this is the will
of God in Christ Jesus for you.
1 Thessalonians 5:16 - 18

Prayer Journal

_____

_____

_____

_____

_____

_____

_____

_____

_____

_____

_____

_____

_____

_____

_____

_____

_____

_____

_____

_____

_____

_____

_____

_____

Prayer Journal

_____

_____

_____

_____

_____

_____

_____

_____

_____

_____

_____

_____

_____

_____

_____

_____

_____

_____

_____

_____

_____

Prayer Journal

Prayer Journal

Prayer Journal

Prayer Journal

Prayer Journal

Prayer Journal

_____

_____

_____

_____

_____

_____

_____

_____

_____

_____

_____

_____

_____

_____

_____

_____

_____

_____

_____

_____

_____

_____

_____

Prayer Journal

Prayer Journal

_____

_____

_____

_____

_____

_____

_____

_____

_____

_____

_____

_____

_____

_____

_____

_____

_____

_____

_____

_____

_____

Prayer Journal

_____

_____

_____

_____

_____

_____

_____

_____

_____

_____

_____

_____

_____

_____

_____

_____

_____

_____

_____

_____

Prayer Journal

Prayer Journal

Prayer Journal

Prayer Journal

_____

_____

_____

_____

_____

_____

_____

_____

_____

_____

_____

_____

_____

_____

_____

_____

_____

_____

_____

_____

_____

_____

Prayer Journal

Prayer Journal

Prayer Journal

Prayer Journal

_____

_____

_____

_____

_____

_____

_____

_____

_____

_____

_____

_____

_____

_____

_____

_____

_____

_____

_____

_____

_____

_____

_____

Prayer Journal

Prayer Journal

Prayer Journal

Prayer Journal

Prayer Journal

Prayer Journal

_____

_____

_____

_____

_____

_____

_____

_____

_____

_____

_____

_____

_____

_____

_____

_____

_____

_____

_____

_____

_____

_____

_____

Prayer Journal

Prayer Journal

_____

_____

_____

_____

_____

_____

_____

_____

_____

_____

_____

_____

_____

_____

_____

_____

_____

_____

_____

_____

_____

_____

_____

Prayer Journal

Prayer Journal

Prayer Journal

_____

_____

_____

_____

_____

_____

_____

_____

_____

_____

_____

_____

_____

_____

_____

_____

_____

_____

_____

_____

_____

_____

Prayer Journal

_____

_____

_____

_____

_____

_____

_____

_____

_____

_____

_____

_____

_____

_____

_____

_____

_____

_____

_____

_____

_____

_____

_____

_____

Prayer Journal

Prayer Journal

Prayer Journal

Prayer Journal

_____

_____

_____

_____

_____

_____

_____

_____

_____

_____

_____

_____

_____

_____

_____

_____

_____

_____

_____

_____

_____

Prayer Journal

Prayer Journal

_____

_____

_____

_____

_____

_____

_____

_____

_____

_____

_____

_____

_____

_____

_____

_____

_____

_____

_____

_____

_____

Prayer Journal

Prayer Journal

Prayer Journal

Prayer Journal

Prayer Journal

Prayer Journal

Prayer Journal

Prayer Journal

_____

_____

_____

_____

_____

_____

_____

_____

_____

_____

_____

_____

_____

_____

_____

_____

_____

_____

_____

_____

_____

_____

Prayer Journal

_____

_____

_____

_____

_____

_____

_____

_____

_____

_____

_____

_____

_____

_____

_____

_____

_____

_____

_____

_____

_____

Prayer Journal

Prayer Journal

_____

_____

_____

_____

_____

_____

_____

_____

_____

_____

_____

_____

_____

_____

_____

_____

_____

_____

_____

_____

_____

_____

_____

_____

Prayer Journal

Prayer Journal

Gratitude Journal

This section of the journal is to record the things in life you are grateful for. Just as we like to hear "thank you" when we have done something for someone, God likes to hear us express our grateful hearts. It is a form of praise! And He is so worthy of our praises!

Take a few moments each day or week to add to the list of things you are grateful for. It can be as simple as the sound of the birds singing to as deep as thanking Him for saving the life of someone you love.

This section of the journal also comes in very handy on those days when everything seems to be going wrong - especially if those days turn into a week, a month, or eight months - and it becomes difficult to express your thankfulness to God. In the seasons when life appears to fall apart, draw upon what you have in this section of your journal to remember the things you are grateful for in the midst of the storm. Read aloud what you have written to express it as a form of praise to God. Before long, you will find you have more to be grateful for than you realized – even in the most difficult of times. You may even be able to add some additional things to your gratitude journal.

Enter into His gates with thanksgiving and into His courts with praise. Be thankful to Him, and bless His name.
Psalm 100:4

Gratitude Journal

_____

_____

_____

_____

_____

_____

_____

_____

_____

_____

_____

_____

_____

_____

_____

_____

_____

_____

_____

_____

Gratitude Journal

_____

_____

_____

_____

_____

_____

_____

_____

_____

_____

_____

_____

_____

_____

_____

_____

_____

_____

_____

_____

_____

Gratitude Journal

Gratitude Journal

_____

_____

_____

_____

_____

_____

_____

_____

_____

_____

_____

_____

_____

_____

_____

_____

_____

_____

_____

_____

_____

Gratitude Journal

Gratitude Journal

Gratitude Journal

_____

_____

_____

_____

_____

_____

_____

_____

_____

_____

_____

_____

_____

_____

_____

_____

_____

_____

_____

Gratitude Journal

Gratitude Journal

Gratitude Journal

_____

_____

_____

_____

_____

_____

_____

_____

_____

_____

_____

_____

_____

_____

_____

_____

_____

_____

_____

_____

_____

Gratitude Journal

_____

_____

_____

_____

_____

_____

_____

_____

_____

_____

_____

_____

_____

_____

_____

_____

_____

_____

_____

_____

Gratitude Journal

_____

_____

_____

_____

_____

_____

_____

_____

_____

_____

_____

_____

_____

_____

_____

_____

_____

_____

_____

_____

_____

_____

Gratitude Journal

_____

_____

_____

_____

_____

_____

_____

_____

_____

_____

_____

_____

_____

_____

_____

_____

_____

_____

_____

Gratitude Journal

_____

_____

_____

_____

_____

_____

_____

_____

_____

_____

_____

_____

_____

_____

_____

_____

_____

_____

_____

_____

_____

Gratitude Journal

Gratitude Journal

Gratitude Journal

Gratitude Journal

Gratitude Journal

_____

_____

_____

_____

_____

_____

_____

_____

_____

_____

_____

_____

_____

_____

_____

_____

_____

_____

_____

Gratitude Journal

Gratitude Journal

Gratitude Journal

_____

_____

_____

_____

_____

_____

_____

_____

_____

_____

_____

_____

_____

_____

_____

_____

_____

_____

_____

_____

_____

Gratitude Journal

Gratitude Journal

_____

_____

_____

_____

_____

_____

_____

_____

_____

_____

_____

_____

_____

_____

_____

_____

_____

_____

_____

_____

_____

Gratitude Journal

_____

_____

_____

_____

_____

_____

_____

_____

_____

_____

_____

_____

_____

_____

_____

_____

_____

_____

_____

_____

Gratitude Journal

Gratitude Journal

Gratitude Journal

Gratitude Journal

_____

_____

_____

_____

_____

_____

_____

_____

_____

_____

_____

_____

_____

_____

_____

_____

_____

_____

_____

_____

Gratitude Journal

Gratitude Journal

Gratitude Journal

Gratitude Journal

Gratitude Journal

Gratitude Journal

Gratitude Journal

Gratitude Journal

_____

_____

_____

_____

_____

_____

_____

_____

_____

_____

_____

_____

_____

_____

_____

_____

_____

_____

_____

_____

Gratitude Journal

Gratitude Journal

_____

_____

_____

_____

_____

_____

_____

_____

_____

_____

_____

_____

_____

_____

_____

_____

_____

_____

_____

_____

_____

Gratitude Journal

Gratitude Journal

_____

_____

_____

_____

_____

_____

_____

_____

_____

_____

_____

_____

_____

_____

_____

_____

_____

_____

_____

_____

_____

Memorable Moments Journal

Of course no journal would be complete without a section to write down your memorable life moments.

So for all those moments you want to remember for years to come or want to share with future generations, go ahead and put them all in here.

Let yourself have the freedom to be creative. Add photos, draw pictures, or do anything else your imagination can come up with.

Were other people part of your memorable moment? Why not have them write down a few things that were special to them? This makes a wonderful memento to reminisce about years down the road.

You will show me the path of life; In Your presence is fullness of joy; At Your right hand are pleasures forevermore.
Psalm 16:11

Memorable Moments Journal

Memorable Moments Journal

Memorable Moments Journal

Memorable Moments Journal

Memorable Moments Journal

Memorable Moments Journal

Memorable Moments Journal

Memorable Moments Journal

Memorable Moments Journal

Memorable Moments Journal

Memorable Moments Journal

Memorable Moments Journal

Memorable Moments Journal

Memorable Moments Journal

Memorable Moments Journal

_____

_____

_____

_____

_____

_____

_____

_____

_____

_____

_____

_____

_____

_____

_____

_____

_____

_____

_____

_____

_____

_____

Memorable Moments Journal

Memorable Moments Journal

Memorable Moments Journal

Memorable Moments Journal

Memorable Moments Journal

Memorable Moments Journal

Memorable Moments Journal

_____

_____

_____

_____

_____

_____

_____

_____

_____

_____

_____

_____

_____

_____

_____

_____

_____

_____

_____

_____

_____

_____

_____

_____

Memorable Moments Journal

Memorable Moments Journal

Memorable Moments Journal

Memorable Moments Journal

Memorable Moments Journal

Memorable Moments Journal

Memorable Moments Journal

Memorable Moments Journal

Memorable Moments Journal

Memorable Moments Journal

Memorable Moments Journal

Memorable Moments Journal

Memorable Moments Journal

Memorable Moments Journal

Memorable Moments Journal

Memorable Moments Journal

Memorable Moments Journal

Memorable Moments Journal

www.ingramcontent.com/pod-product-compliance
Lightning Source LLC
Chambersburg PA
CBHW070840100426
42813CB00003B/685